Purchased through a nutrition and health grant
generous

Pa

May, 2004

LIVING WITH
CEREBRAL PALSY

Paul Pimm

RSVP
RAINTREE
STECK-VAUGHN
PUBLISHERS
A Steck-Vaughn Company

Austin, Texas

www.steck-vaughn.com

Our Lady of the Lake University
411 S.W. 24th St.
San Antonio, TX 78207
(210) 434-6711

Titles in the series

Living with Asthma
Living with Blindness
Living with Cerebral Palsy
Living with Deafness
Living with Diabetes
Living with Down Syndrome
Living with Epilepsy
Living with Leukemia

© Copyright 2000, text, Steck-Vaughn Company

All rights reserved. No part of this book may be reproduced or utilized in any form or by any means, electronic or mechanical, including photocopying, recording, or by any information storage and retrieval system, without permission in writing from the Publisher. Inquiries should be addressed to: Copyright Permissions, Steck-Vaughn Company, P.O. Box 26015, Austin, TX 78755.

Published by Raintree Steck-Vaughn Publishers, an imprint of Steck-Vaughn Company

Library of Congress Cataloging-in-Publication Data
Pimm, Paul.
Living with cerebral palsy / Paul Pimm.
     p.   cm.—(Living with)
     Includes bibliographical references and index.
     Summary: Describes the varying effects of cerebral palsy, how different people manage to live with this condition, and where to get more information.
     ISBN 0-8172-5744-6
     1. Cerebral palsy—Juvenile literature.
     [1. Cerebral palsy.]
     I. Title. II. Title: Cerebral palsy
     RC388.P56   1999
     362.1'96836—dc21   99-27202

Printed in Italy. Bound in the United States.
1 2 3 4 5 6 7 8 9 0 03 02 01 00 99

Picture acknowledgments
The publishers would like to thank: Angela Hampton *cover* [inset], 10, 27, 29; Tony Stone/Laurence Dutton 26, /Richard Shock 8; Science Photo Library/Alfred Pasieka 11. All the other photographs were taken by Martyn F. Chillmaid.

Contents

Meet Katie, Jenny, Paul, and Simon

Katie, Jenny, and Paul are children, just like you. They live with their parents, and they go to school, have friends, and enjoy doing many activities. Simon is older and has just started work.

Katie is nine years old. Her hobby is an unusual one. She keeps different kinds of fish from all around the world. One day, Katie hopes to go scuba diving to see the fish in the sea.

◁ Jenny loves animals. She has a dog, three cats, a rabbit, and a hamster.

△ Katie has mild cerebral palsy, and she can do most things her friends can do.

Jenny is eleven years old. She lives with her parents on a farm, where she sometimes helps out with work. She loves the springtime when she can help feed the baby lambs.

▷ Paul has joined his school swimming club. Swimming is one of the best exercises he can do.

Paul is twelve years old. His favorite hobby is swimming. One of his arms and one leg do not work very well, but this does not keep him from enjoying himself with his friends.

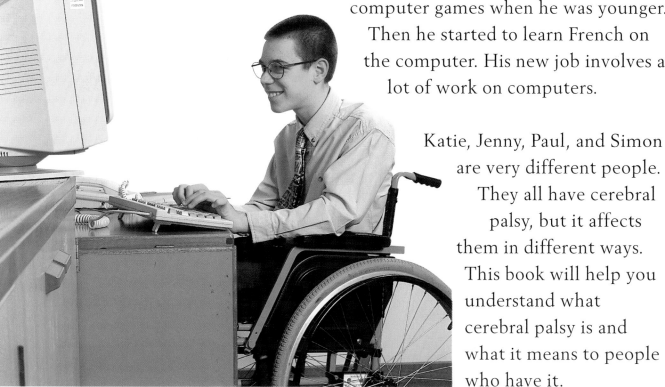

▽ Simon always wanted to work with computers.

Simon is eighteen years old, and he's just started his first job after leaving school. He worked very hard at his exams so that he would be able to get a good job. Simon has always loved computers. He began by playing computer games when he was younger. Then he started to learn French on the computer. His new job involves a lot of work on computers.

Katie, Jenny, Paul, and Simon are very different people. They all have cerebral palsy, but it affects them in different ways. This book will help you understand what cerebral palsy is and what it means to people who have it.

The Brain and Cerebral Palsy

Your brain is in charge of your body. It tells your body what to do and how to do it. For example, it tells you to breathe, it tells your heart to beat, and it tells your arms and legs to move. Many parts of the brain are involved in making a movement. When you want to kick a ball, the brain sends a message to your leg, telling it what to do.

When someone has cerebral palsy, part of the brain is not working very well. Messages to the muscles that control movement are not sent properly or are jumbled. As a result the person's movements might be jerky or their muscles stiff. He or she might stand or sit awkwardly.

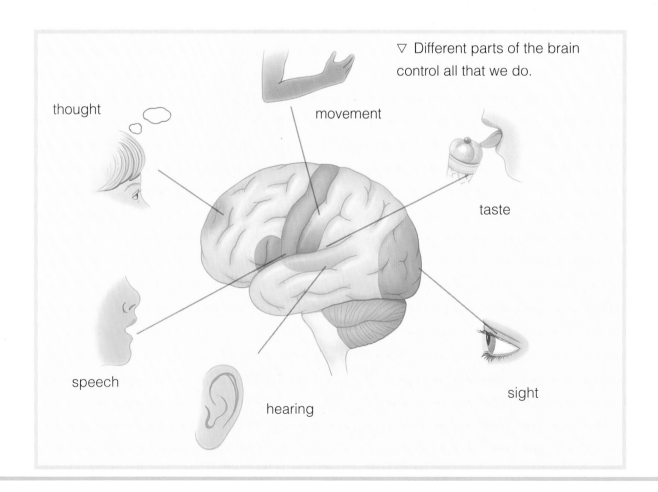

∇ Different parts of the brain control all that we do.

thought

movement

taste

speech

hearing

sight

Not everyone with cerebral palsy is affected in the same way. Some people are only affected in small ways that may not be noticed. Others may have problems using their arms and legs. Talking or even chewing and swallowing may be difficult.

Sometimes the brain cannot easily work out what it sees, so people have problems understanding patterns and shapes. For some people, doing a jigsaw, tying a shoelace, judging distances, or catching a ball may be difficult. For others, reading or doing math may be hard. The rest of the brain may work perfectly well. Having cerebral palsy does not keep Katie, Jenny, and Paul from having fun and joining in many activities. It did not stop Simon from getting a good job.

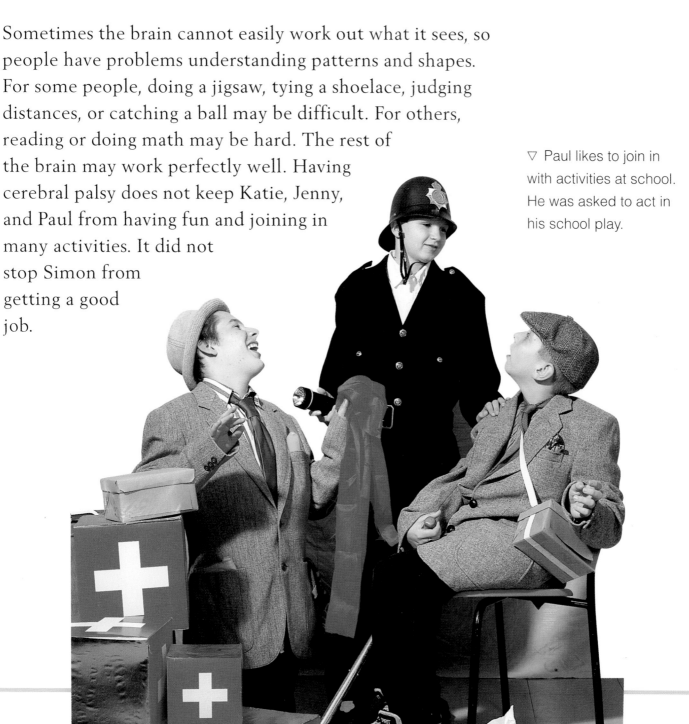

▽ Paul likes to join in with activities at school. He was asked to act in his school play.

Why Cerebral Palsy Happens

Cerebral palsy can happen in any family, in boys and girls, and in any country. It happens before birth, around the time of birth, or in early childhood, as a result of part of the brain not developing properly or getting damaged. Sometimes it is possible to find out why this happens. It might be because of bleeding or blocked blood vessels in the brain, problems during birth, or because a baby was born much too soon.

▽ This young baby is in an incubator. She would not live without the help of this machine. The doctor is checking her condition.

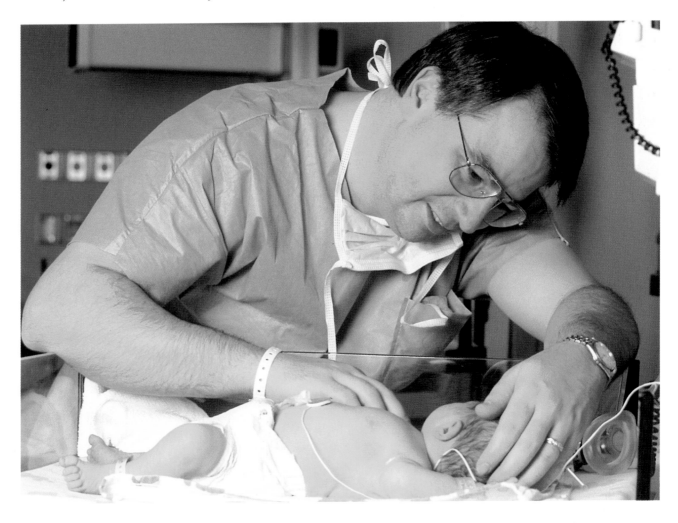

▷ Having cerebral palsy does not mean that your own children will have it.

Sometimes infections in the brain such as meningitis can cause cerebral palsy. It can be inherited, but this is very rare. Often, no one knows why someone has cerebral palsy.

It is usually very difficult to find out why a person develops cerebral palsy. Simon's doctor could not be sure. This worried his mother and father a lot when he was younger, but it did not matter to Simon. Simon is very happy with his life and his new job. Having cerebral palsy doesn't keep him from doing what he wants to do.

Finding Out About It

Sometimes the doctor knows that a baby is unwell before it is born. An ultrasound scan may be taken so that a doctor can see the baby inside his or her mother. This test helps the doctor check the health of the baby.

At other times doctors may not be sure of a baby's health until he or she is born. The baby's parents may be the first to notice that something is wrong, because they spend most of their time with their child. They may notice that the baby is not eating or moving properly. A person who is specially trained in problems that affect the brain, called a neurologist, may be asked to help. Doctors may watch a baby for a long time and may take a scan of the baby's brain in order to find out what is wrong.

▽ An ultrasound scan helps the doctor see how well the unborn baby is developing.

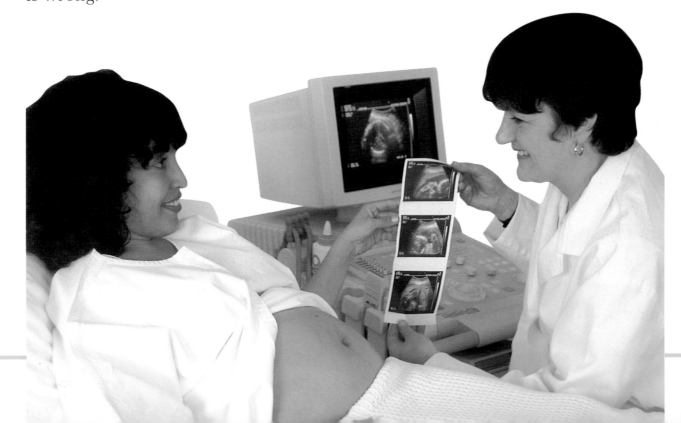

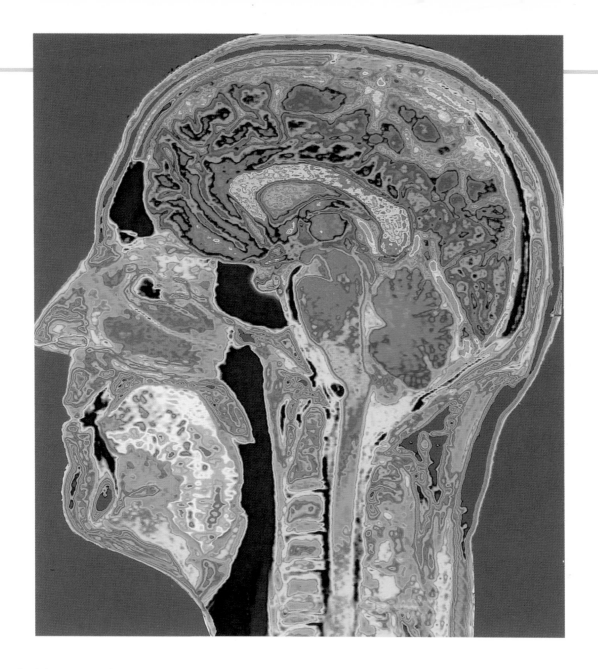

Some children with cerebral palsy may have learning difficulties. Others may have epilepsy. Some may have severe speech, sight, or hearing problems. If the doctor thinks that a person has epilepsy, a special test called an EEG might be done. This does not hurt. Sticky pads with wires are attached to the head to pick up messages sent out by the brain. The test helps the doctor decide whether a person has epilepsy. The doctor will then tell the person and his or her parents about the best way to treat the condition.

△ This picture of a healthy brain was produced by an MRI scan.

Treatment

There is no cure for cerebral palsy, but with the right treatment life can be made much better. Physical exercises help many people develop better movements and may also ease stiffness. Sometimes an operation may be needed to help people move more easily or to help ease pain or discomfort. Medicine may also help relax the stiff muscles.

Jenny has a speech therapist because she has difficulty speaking. When Jenny first started her speaking exercises, she did not like them. Now Jenny feels more confident about talking, and she feels a lot happier. She has a nickname of Chatterbox at school now.

△ Jenny's speech is getting better with the help of speech therapy.

Simon has difficulty walking. He uses a wheelchair a lot of the time, but his physiotherapist likes him to be on his feet for part of the day. This gives him some exercise, and it keeps the blood moving properly in his legs.

Paul has to take medicine every day to control his epilepsy and to stop having seizures. Sometimes it can take a while to find the right medicine and the right amount to take. Paul used to feel tired, and his schoolwork suffered. His doctor changed the amount of medicine Paul was taking, and soon he was fine again.

Katie walks quite well, but she may have an operation on her leg to make walking easier.

Some people with cerebral palsy have problems with their eyes. The most common problem is a squint, which can be helped with glasses or an operation. Sometimes there might be a problem with hearing, and a hearing aid may help. Cerebral palsy doesn't get worse as you get older. However, someone with the condition can feel the effects of growing older earlier.

△ Before the doors were widened at his home, Simon could not get his wheelchair through the door very easily.

People Who Can Help

There are many people whose jobs involve helping others with difficulties. When someone has cerebral palsy, he or she can receive help and advice so that life can be made better.

A child with cerebral palsy will usually be looked after by a doctor called a pediatrician, who is specially trained to treat the health problems of children. He or she will advise parents on the type of care needed for their child.

▽ The occupational therapist is showing Jenny the best way to use the special spoon, so she can eat without help.

Children with learning difficulties may need special help in school from an educational psychologist. Sometimes a child may have problems learning to read or with drawing or math. The child may be very smart, but needs extra time to learn some things. Educational psychologists visit schools and advise teachers on the best way they can help.

Cerebral palsy can mean that some people have problems doing everyday things, such as brushing teeth, bathing, or getting around. For an older person with cerebral palsy, cooking and cleaning may be difficult. An occupational therapist can give advice on special equipment that will help.

▷ A physiotherapist is showing Simon how to stretch his legs. It is important to do exercises throughout your life.

It can be hard to move properly when muscles do not work very well. With help from a physiotherapist, who can advise on exercises to do and how to move, movement can be made easier.

Some people have difficulty talking, and their speech is not very clear. Others may have problems with sucking, swallowing, and chewing, and they may dribble. A speech and language therapist can help with these problems.

Everyday life

Katie, Jenny, Paul, and Simon are affected in different ways by their cerebral palsy, but some of the problems they face are the same. Parents like to protect their children, but sometimes they can overdo it, as Jenny discovered. Jenny is in a wheelchair and has some problems with speech. Her parents were afraid to let her go anywhere without them, but now they know that Jenny is sensible and will ask for help when she needs it.

▽ Sometimes parents need to be careful. Katie's parents need to watch her, but she is allowed to play outside with her friends.

△ Simon likes to talk about his day with his parents in the evening.

When Simon was younger, he did not go out without his parents. Life got better when he got older. He would go out with his friends to a movie or for a meal. Being in a wheelchair does not keep Simon from having a life of his own, but he will always be grateful to his parents for their love and care. Simon has just passed his driving test, so he can drive to work and visit his friends.

Paul has epilepsy, and his mother was afraid to let him go out without her, in case he had a seizure. A specially trained epilepsy nurse explained how important it was that Paul join in as much as possible. The nurse talked to his friends about Paul's condition and showed them how to help if he did have a seizure. Paul and his parents feel much happier now.

Katie at School

There may be some children at your school who have physical problems or difficulties with learning. Katie goes to an ordinary school. She has learning difficulties and needs extra time to learn most things. She has a special classroom helper to help with her lessons.

Katie has mild cerebral palsy, so she can play most games and sports. There is a girl in a wheelchair in Katie's class. She doesn't have cerebral palsy. She was in an accident and injured her legs. Katie gets along with her, but Katie gets along with everyone. The teacher says it's because Katie is nosy and likes to know everything.

▽ Katie gets extra help so she can keep up with the rest of her class.

18

◁ Katie is a bit of a daredevil and will try anything.

I really like sports

"I like running. I fall over sometimes, but I don't hurt myself. I love swimming most of all. My physiotherapist says it is good for me, so I ask Mom to take me every day on the school breaks."

When Katie first started school, some of the children teased her about the way she walked. Katie did not understand why they were doing this, and she got very upset. One day, she came home crying. It took her mother a long time to find out what was wrong. Katie's friend, Sonia, told Katie's mother, who then spoke to Katie's teacher about it. The teacher soon sorted it out, and now anyone at the school who is being teased can get help. Some of the older children help the younger ones who are being teased by talking about the problem with them.

Jenny at Boarding School

Jenny is affected by cerebral palsy much more than Katie, Paul, and Simon. Jenny goes to a boarding school. Her parents live in the country, and it's a long way from her nearest school. Some children do not like the idea of going away to school, but Jenny liked it after she went on a visit. She stays there all the time, apart from school vacations and some weekends when her parents take her home.

△ Jenny's parents told the teacher how much Jenny is enjoying school now.

My first school trip

"I went on a school trip this year to France on the train. I needed a bit of extra support, so the lady who helps me in class came along as well."

△ The electric wheelchair means that Jenny can move around easily. But she gets uncomfortable if she sits in it all day.

Jenny likes the dog that sits at the front door of the school and makes a fuss of everyone as they come in. It belongs to the principal. She also likes the swimming pool. She swims every day as part of her exercises.

Her parents like the school because Jenny can have daily physical exercises to improve her movement, and speech therapy, which helps Jenny speak more clearly. Jenny also has a lot of extra help in the classroom.

When Jenny started school, she was homesick for a while and came home most weekends. Jenny now stays the whole term because there are lots of things to do with her friends at school.

Simon at Work

While Simon was still at school, he was able to try some work experience. The career adviser found him a temporary job in a big computer company. Simon was nervous at first, but everyone was very friendly. It was a large office with plenty of space, so Simon could use his wheelchair if he wanted to. He liked the experience so much that he decided to work on computers when he left school.

◁ Simon can drive to work now that he has passed his driving test. Cars can be specially adapted for people's needs.

Simon did very well in his exams at school. He could have gone to college, but he wanted to work. He remembered the company where he did his work experience, and he wrote to the manager to find out whether there was any work available. The manager remembered Simon, and, after an interview, he gave him a job.

In his first week, Simon put information into the computer and could not find it when it was needed. Simon thought he would lose his job. He did not, but he soon learned how important it was to do things carefully. Now he is enjoying his job very much.

Exams at work

"I was surprised that I had to keep studying, even after I started work. I thought that exams had finished at school."

▷ Simon worked hard at his exams, which helped him get a job.

Looking Ahead

▽ It may take some children much longer to learn physical skills such as walking and crawling.

There is no cure for cerebral palsy, but, with the right treatment and support from an early age, many children will go on to lead busy and happy lives. Some will go to college. Others may go to work after leaving school, and some will have their own children. Some of the jobs that people with cerebral palsy do include working with computers, office work, and social work.

For those with the most serious problems, support can be given to help them be as independent as possible. Someone in a wheelchair with very little movement in his or her hands would be able to drive an electric wheelchair. They could turn on the television, draw the curtains, open and close the door, or program their VCR. If they had no speech, they could use an electronic voice. All this is possible with the use of computers. In the future, science will allow people to do even more for themselves.

▷ People with very little movement can lead their own lives. If they cannot do much for themselves, they can tell other people how to help them.

Katie, Jenny, Paul, and Simon want people to understand a little about cerebral palsy. They do not want people to feel sorry for them or to be embarrassed because they have cerebral palsy. Remember, people with cerebral palsy have the same needs as other people. They want to be loved, have fun, be supported, and have the chance to learn about the world.

Getting Help

If you, one of your friends, or someone in your family has cerebral palsy, there are several organizations you can contact. They will be able to give you advice and may be able to put you in touch with other people who have cerebral palsy.

▽ Different organizations can give advice on education and schools.

United Cerebral Palsy is the second largest health charity in America. The organization's mission is to advance the independence of people with cerebral palsy. UCP has chapters throughout the country. Each local group offers therapy, technological training, family support programs, social and recreational programs, and employment assistance. UCP is the leading source of information on cerebral palsy in the country. You can contact United Cerebral Palsy at 1600 L Street NW, Suite 700; Washington, DC 20036-5602 or at their web site at www.ucpa.org.

American Academy for Cerebral Palsy and Developmental Medicine (AACPDM) is a scientific society dedicated to the study of cerebral palsy. The society has committees and programs through which it promotes education for treatment and management of the disease, as well as working to improve the quality of life of those with cerebral palsy. AACPDM publishes a newsletter, and its web site features an updated library of informational materials for parents and professionals. You can write AACPDM at 6300 North River Road, Suite 727; Rosemont, IL 60018-4226 or at their web site at www.aacpdm.org.

The Cerebral Palsy Network is an organization of parents who are concerned with the ways in which children and their families are affected by cerebral palsy. The group provides help and advice for parents on how to raise children with cerebral palsy and what to expect from them. They have established an online support group for the exchange of experiences and information. Future plans for the network are the establishment of a volunteer-staffed clinic for cerebral palsy patients, and the creation of an equipment bank. You can write the Cerebral Palsy Network at 1448 Goldenrod S.E.; Lacey, WA 98513 or at their web site at www.geocities.com/Heartland/Plains/8950.

△ There are organizations that can help give advice on equipment to suit special needs.

Glossary

Brain An organ inside the head that controls everything that we do by passing messages to the nerves.

EEG A test that records the messages sent out by the brain, to try to pick up any abnormal activity. EEG is short for electroencephalogram.

Epilepsy A condition caused by chemical disturbances in the brain that cause seizures.

Hemiplegia A condition in which one side of the body is paralyzed.

Meningitis A serious disease that causes inflammation of the membranes covering the brain and spinal cord.

MRI scan A test that uses a very strong magnet to pick up signals from a person's brain. These signals are then fed into a computer so that a picture of the brain can be made. MRI is short for Magnetic Resonance Imaging.

Muscles Strong tissue composed of fibers that can get shorter and longer and so produce movements of the body.

Neurologist A doctor specially trained to treat problems that affect the brain.

Occupational therapist A person who is specially trained to help people with movement and give advice on special equipment.

Pediatrician A doctor who is specially trained to treat health problems affecting children.

Physiotherapist A person who is specially trained to help people move more easily, for example, by showing them what exercises to do.

Seizure A problem caused when messages being sent to the brain get muddled. There are several types of seizures.

Squint An eye that turns in a different way from the other eye.

Further information

Organizations

See pages 28 and 29 for the names and addresses of organizations specializing in cerebral palsy.

Books to Read

Fiction

Metzger, Lois. *Barry's Sister*. New York: Atheneum Books for Young Readers, 1992.

———. *Ellen's Case*. New York: Puffin Books, 1997.

Mikaelson, Ben. *Petey*. New York: Hyperion Press, 1998.

Information Books

Brannon, Dan. *The Courage to Live: Doune Gustavel's Triumph Over Cerebral Palsy and Deafness*. Don Brauman Publications, 1997.

Geralis, Elaine, ed. *Children with Cerebral Palsy: A Parent's Guide*. Bethesda, MD: Woodbine House, 1998.

Mann, Gary, et. al. *Everybody Is Special*. Macon, GA: Mercer University Press, 1995.

Index

Page numbers in **bold** refer to pictures as well as text.

© Copyright 1999 Wayland (Publishers) Ltd.